Intimate and lovely, the poems of Tyler Robert Sheldon allow us to appreciate the small, overlooked wonders of our familiar worlds. In Sheldon's poems, there's great compassion for people, for landscapes, for family members, and for an unromanticized past. In this poet's work, it's the little things that count—moments of conversation, kitchen windows, the flights of native birds, the "sea ghosts" of Kansas. [Sheldon] writes frequently of an overlooked Midwestern state—Kansas—and a storied Southern one—Louisiana—with an exacting eye for detail and a sense of earned wonder. In *Driving Together*, we encounter a poetic voice that will take us into the heart of each destination, and it's a joy to hear this voice unwind in these fine and succinct poems.

> ~ Allison Joseph, author of
> *Confessions of a Barefaced Woman*

Not many poets can bridge the wild terrain between lemons, ghosts of an inland sea, semiotics, a hurricane, and a coyote howling in the Flint Hills of Kansas, but Tyler Sheldon, in his first full-length collection of poetry, speaks directly and distinctly to the everyday realities and deep-night mysteries of life. *Driving Together* invites the reader to climb on for a ride across vistas of land and language, picking up speed by reading the omens along the way, and slowing down just in time to arrive at new understandings of home and adventure. His writing is clear-eyed and precise while embracing a wide vista of time and place. As he writes in "Elegy," "This poem believes / in extinction, knows / blades and grass keep / secrets just like us." Come drive together with Sheldon to find the more expansive view of our lives made visible in the quiet and original heart of these poems.

> ~ Caryn Mirriam-Goldberg, 2009-2013 Kansas Poet Laureate, author of *Everyday Magic: Field Notes on the Mundane and Miraculous*

Tyler Sheldon performs a young poet's affection for formative experience recollected in early manhood, seasoned with a mischievous whimsy.

~ Steven Hind, author of *The Loose Change of Wonder*

Tyler Robert Sheldon's *Driving Together* excavates a family history and maps its place in Kansas with a storyteller's mind and a poet's precision. These poem's honor Sheldon's identical twin brother who died after a "small handful of hours," and give a language for the spaces we make for the lives that were too short: "I see you behind my eyelids, and touch / you as I pluck a leaf from concrete." Sheldon writes to illuminate how loss defines a place—"Our best scenery / is not on the ground"—and in doing so, preserves what is fleeting.

~ Ruth Awad, author of *Set to Music a Wildfire*

Driving Together by Tyler Robert Sheldon is a dynamic book of verse that celebrates life through love: fraternal love, romantic love, love for mindfulness, love for nature, love for writing. In its lines, the poet confesses his greatest fears, but they are released along with the breath the reader exhales when each syllable is pronounced; likewise, it is there where the poetic voice and the reader intersect in a journey of words that can be read peacefully time after time: "...The record will spin like the passing world...We'll listen again—as many times as we need." In these pages, the poet holds an inner dialogue with himself, guiding the reader through the poetic voice's rite of passage. With each verse, Sheldon's voice matures, reaching a catharsis in the end. The present moment is full of creative energy through which the poet continues his life journey, "his ears alert, his eyes full of wind and moon." This is a book I will read again and again.

~Xánath Caraza, Writer-in-Residence, Westchester Community College, New York

DRIVING TOGETHER

POEMS

TYLER ROBERT SHELDON

Meadowlark (an imprint of Chasing Tigers Press)
meadowlark-books.com
P.O. Box 333, Emporia, KS 66801

Copyright © 2018 Tyler Robert Sheldon

All rights reserved. This book or any portion thereof
may not be reproduced or used in any manner whatsoever
without the express written permission of the author
except for the use of brief quotations in a book review.

Cover Photo & Author Photo by Alex Arceneaux

ISBN: 978-1-7322410-0-8

Library of Congress Control Number: 2018941186

Driving Together

POEMS

Tyler Robert Sheldon

A MEADOWLARK BOOK

*For Alex Arceneaux, with whom I have found
a truer poetry than any other I have known*

CONTENTS

FOREWORD BY KEVIN RABAS

I. LEMONS

Replay 3
Lemons 4
Driveway Olympics 5
August 6
My Father Teaches Me to Shave 7
Mountains 8

II. UNIVERSAL SOLVENTS

Brother 11
Universal Solvents 12
Discovering a Lost Twin 13
If You're Listening 14
Guitar 15
Photo of Brother 16
Scar 17
Gravity 18

III. SEA GHOSTS OF KANSAS

In Kansas 21
Code 22
Red-Tails 23
Discovering 24
Sea Ghosts of Kansas 25
For Kansas Poets 26
Satori 27
Negotiations 28
Showing Off 29
To See How Surrealists 30
Recipe, Condensed 31

Watching Sky 32
Home 33
Elegy 34
Elmer has the perfect truck 35

IV. DRIVING TOGETHER

Buying the Ford 39
Ablution 40
First Weekend After Snow: Emporia, Kansas 41
After Long John Silver's 42
Semiotics 43
At the End of Graduate School 44
Waking After the Wreck 45
Get Lost 46
After a Crash 47

V. SOUTH

Louisiana Aubade 51
When to Run From a Hurricane 52
Yardwork 53
Dead Man Fingers 54
At the Court of Two Sisters 56

VI. WHEN NEXT WE MEET

Catharsis 59
Finding Yourself 60

NOTES
PUBLICATION CREDITS
ACKNOWLEDGMENTS
ABOUT THE AUTHOR

Foreword

Tyler Robert Sheldon's first full-length poetry collection *Driving Together* is a gem, a culmination of years of study and effort. As an MA student Tyler impressively published more than forty poems individually, demonstrating both his industry and his ambition, his talent and grit. With his MFA in Creative Writing currently in progress and this book complete, Tyler takes the next step as a poet and educator. With this collection, his audience and reach quickly extend.

Tyler's life is both ordinary and extraordinary, and he charts some of his journey in verse in this book. He does so with hope and pluck, with a kind of simple, clear vision. What he sees, we see. One instance is his adventurous elopement with his artist love Alexandria, which includes a ceremony in Emporia, Kansas's Peter Pan Park not far from the spot where his infant twin's ashes were scattered, a bittersweet mix of joy and sorrow, hope and grief. Much of the book is tempered in this way, where youthful car cruising turns into a momentous car wreck, Tyler roused from his crinkled car. A quiet breakfast with his parents turns to metaphor, the egg in the skillet like the lost brother's amorphous body and brain.

Also, there is the music. Tyler, a gifted guitarist, imagines heaven as a record store, where he drops the needle down and the record "spin(s) like the passing world," and we listen "as many times as we need." In this poem and others, there's a sense of nostalgia: a hopeful, but never saccharine, lens on the passage of time. As an artist, during recent years Tyler has learned to chisel and hone his work, his words. Like a boxer's body, his verses are now lean and mean, but also supple, liquid-quick, where "every cloud / shudders like a gong" and "This poem believes / in extinction, knows / blades and grass keep / secrets just like us."

In these lines and others, there's a sense of discovery, how in simple observation one can find the natural metaphor of the moment—and metaphor no one may have ever found before: gong/cloud and secret-keeping grass. Such are the mysteries of existence, and Tyler works to unearth them. Through his looking, his vision, we learn.

Enjoy this collection—and its secrets, its observations. I know I have.

>   Kevin Rabas
>   Poet Laureate of Kansas
>   2017-2019

LEMONS

REPLAY

When my time spins around,
I will return as a record store clerk
and customers will come and ask,
"Hey, man, what do you recommend?"
I'll say try this one.

I'll put on the album I've picked
and drop the needle-arm down.
The record will spin like the passing world.
When it reaches the end I'll flip the LP over.
We'll listen again—as many times as we need.

LEMONS

As a baby I'm told I ate lemons,
grinding pulp between nubby teeth,
spitting seeds to the wind
or the garden overgrown
with yellow marigolds.

Our Schnauzer ate
gummy Payday candy bars,
peanuts in his sharp doggy teeth
while my parents painted
the kitchen yellow.

The neighbors' fence became my spot
for cold, cold ice cream or small padded books,
and led to the faded yellow tetherball
out back before I knew about the owner's
cheating, his wife's insanity. Even then
I was across the street anyway,
in the middle of Oz,
so I was safe.

The street corner's giant wooden bear
kept me safe on walks
through our neighborhood.
I would sail yellow paper ships
in the backyard pool,
make vinegar volcanoes,
be a kid because I was good at it,
and liked it that way.

DRIVEWAY OLYMPICS

"In 1988, Jamaica took part in the Calgary, Canada Winter Olympics. They competed in only one sport: bobsledding."
-The Jamaican Bobsleigh Federation, 2008

The sled hits
the end of our concrete
gauntlet, clacking on ice,
the crispness of December,
the orange burst of childhood.

Feel the rhythm,
Hear the rhyme.
Dad's behind me
as we schlep the sled
to the top of the driveway,
our starting line.

He pushes the sled.
I fall to the street.
My fingers tighten
on rope, waiting
for gravel, impact,
my father's words:

Come on, Jamaica.
It's bobsled time.

AUGUST

My father walks, leaden
pipe in hand (dog insurance).
Down street
the Akita runs a length
of iron chain.

Seeds explode like fire
against the neighbor's garage.

I am barefoot and fifteen
on hot concrete.
The mail truck pulls away
into the hallucinatory shimmer
of street.

I breathe
once, and run
for the box
with all I have.

My Father Teaches Me to Shave

Near bedtime, I sit
on the high lip of the tub.
You stand shirtless at the mirror
trimming split ends from a beard
going gray.

I am not yet five.
My feet don't reach the floor
but I ask to shave, to be a man,
so you hand me the can of foam,
and tell me, "Rub some on your face."

You see the razor has no blade,
and focus sharply as we guide it
through the foam. Afterward,
we marvel at the smoothness
of my cheeks, the astringent tingle.

You say I'm a man now.
I feel tall enough for the counter,
where we both reflect
in that big mirror.

Mountains

Driving us up to his mountain cabin,
my grandfather tells me
how his father owned a liquor store
here in Colorado, how
he'd run the bar up front like a ship's captain,
throw overboard belligerent folk
who'd had too much.
He'd chuck 'em right out the door,
my grandpa chuckled,
because he was a boxer, and a damn good one.
People knew not to mess around.

Grandpa tells me I would've liked his father,
who'd had a baseball field named after him
here in Colorado, because he could
pitch so fast you'd never see the ball,
and the hands of the batter and catcher
would be numb for hours.
Both often just got out of the way.

I'd be proud of his father, he says.
We turn further into the mountains
He was a bootlegger, you know,
smuggling booze in hat and overcoat.
He didn't care what folks thought.

You'd like him, Grandpa says,
because you're just like him.
I look at him there in the driver's seat,
and he smiles back at me.
I know he is right.

Universal Solvents

BROTHER

". . . able to touch your heart like a leaf."
                            —Jimmy Santiago Baca

You, with the cluster of hospital tubes
held too loose in your premature blood,
your small felt hat in a closet box
that squats out of sight like a fist.
You, who left me breathing alone.

You, sitting in Peter Pan Park
in leaf-scattered morning sun.
You, whose spinal fluid broke all rules
and made its own cranial walls.
You, whom I will always understand
just as well as myself, and not at all.

I feel you in the back muscle twinges
that cling me to bed in the morning.
I see you behind my eyelids, and touch
you as I pluck a leaf from concrete
when my left hand is free.

Universal Solvents

At six I dreamt of drowning,
sinking under black ocean,
a giant white shark pulling me
to surface air, dragging
himself back to water while
I pleaded his company;
his journey was only
to stay down.

At breakfast, my parents said
that shark had been a boy
who'd looked like me, didn't
make it. Mom's hand shook, broke
yolks in skillet. Long minutes passed
before I spoke.

I learned new ideas, words: fluidity,
brain cavity, undeveloped,
flat line. Twins. How one half
of a pair can forfeit, as in swimming:
let the other touch beach first,
and drown. His face

matching mine, I see only
a white shark sinking,
or a small doomed skillet,
broken brain spilling
over tiny spoon of skull.

DISCOVERING A LOST TWIN

When a giant shark comes to you
in the night, glowing and shrieking
that ocean mammal binary

that you don't know logically,
but can somehow still connect with
on some hidden level of the amygdala,

is your first impulse to swim
away? Would you listen as it tells you
it's here to save you from drowning

in the dark ocean that suddenly
and ominously surrounds you?
Would you grasp for its pale fins

as it pulls you toward light?
Would you try simply
to wake up?

If You're Listening

brother
I have written poems about you
because I don't really know
who you are now and because
I want to know so badly
it makes my teeth ache

Did you know my wife and I
got married in the park
where you were scattered
after you stayed for
your small handful of hours

of course you know

    you were there

I've read about mystic women
and men who can check
on those like you
who've moved away
from the rest of us

but I don't really know
if I'm ready yet

you're probably playing guitar
and running fingers   through
your red hair

is your beard dark red like mine

do you ever laugh for an hour
because you can't help yourself

    sometimes I do

GUITAR

Right now my brother is probably
learning how it feels to write his first song.
It would be about the shock of rain
on his fresh-shaven face, my own age.
He is just learning to hold down the strings
so they don't muffle his beautiful sound.

He loves major chords. He tries to fret
C and D and E. He even asks me
for advice: *you've played since we
were kids, could you show me this?*
I take the polished neck
from a hand just like my own,
and finger a chord, my index
spanning two strings.

He practices for hours. We sit together
as he holds the strings down.
When he masters each chord,
the rain falls from his smooth face
and into the wet ground.

Photo of Brother
scattered in Peter Pan Park, Emporia, Kansas

Within my head I am not alone
But am grateful for the lack of stone
That marks my mirror in the wind,
His final place, where I begin
To meet the boy I've barely known.

This little hand, so like my own,
These tiny shoes for tiny bones
This dark mirage: my only twin,
Within my head.

Sometimes when I pick up the phone
I hope to hear him and atone
For my long held survivor's sin.
I owe him all that might have been.
I hear my brother, fully grown,
Within my head.

SCAR

At school, the other boys
mock me in the freshman
locker room.   I tell them
I'm the bionic man. They
know only how to breathe
through lungs that opened
and closed like bellows
since the day they were born.

In physical therapy, I learn
to ignore it through sit-ups
that stretch it like a smile
at my side. Later

I embrace it, run fingers
along puckered rib-skin
in the shower, breathe
deep because I can,
because through my ribs
is the metal holding tight
my lungs, the best hospitals
could do for a boy born
too early for much other
than prayer. While my scar

is still here, my brother
(three hours long for
our world) became his own,
spinal fluid scalding
his broken brain. It

reminds me memories
don't fade with age,
and some stretch to fit
the holes we make
in our hearts.

GRAVITY

The chortle some birds make when afraid to fly
before their parents boot them to the ground for the first time
and they piece together that they'd better figure this out quick
isn't laughter but instead
realization that the world hates waiting.

Swifts, ocean birds that stay up
for years at a time and sleep on the wing,
don't ask how it all works because
maybe if they did it wouldn't anymore
and thousands of birds would fall
like comets into the sea.

No matter how they try
                                  some birds can't fly.

Sea Ghosts of Kansas

IN KANSAS

if you're not impressed,
don't sweat it. Our best scenery
is not on the ground.

Start slow. Go drag Main
in a rusted-out car.
Eat fish sandwiches from soggy wrappers
with no-good tartar sauce;
throw clove cigarette butts into the street.

Walk dirt roads because you can;
search for ruby slippers.
Take in the wagon-wheel mailboxes,
the six-hundred-foot salt mines.

Throw lines into the air.
Fish kites from the paling sky.

CODE

In the Flint Hills
when walking, touch
the bluestem half-
way down the blade
to feel a finished thought
not yet in words.

Wait for squirrels
to make it halfway
up the cottonwoods
before approaching, and
don't look for redemption.

In these hills,
you make your own.

RED-TAILS

Eastern Kansas. Red-tails
perch on posts, like mobsters:
  "one boid, two boid."
  From the road,
we marvel at the fat
who have earned it,
who lease sky
to leaner chests, sharper
wings. Hawks know
who's boss.

DISCOVERING

the way a hummingbird
alters its dizzying flight by degrees,
flits up, back and away,
undoes itself.

How cicadas, like teens,
oversleep, never ask
to borrow the car
or stay out late,
but then wake up,
break the rules,
drone into sky.

And the bracket of geese
which wings itself across clouds
each evening, changing leads:
a great self-winding watch
which ticks and shifts its way
through a band of stars.

SEA GHOSTS OF KANSAS

Out here
on the plains none of us
really know all that much
about what we're doing, and
in this sea ghost of tall grass
we call home,
the smallest rocks and
calcified shellfish which
come into our sandals and homes
are comforting and disarming
in the same breath. We are
the dubiously welcome
newcomers here, and not just
to any ancient people.
It's worth remembering
no one's all that ancient. Once
if you didn't have gills
then what the hell
after all
were you doing
out here

FOR KANSAS POETS

This act may not seem writing
so much as incision
into the limestone of this place,
where you sit alone in dark pre-morning
static while long-necked turbines
stride the paling edge
of sky, blading the ancient clouds
into white rope while the wheat
or Bluestem—sargassum clasping thought—
crashes upon rocks, themselves
grasping fossils in veins of Florence
chert, words newly tied to the page
waiting until next you breathe,
calling them, wind through leaves.

SATORI

To be happy you should understand
that everything you've ever done
up to now is a screen door swinging
on one hinge. In the middle
of its gauzy wire there's a hole
where maybe a cat clung one evening
and is now long since far and away
from here. Maybe a passing car
kicked up a rock. Either way
it now belongs to the evening sun
which reaches its long fingers
to touch you. To be happy
is to say that maybe the door
was always this way.

NEGOTIATIONS

Back door open, the black Lab
gallops toward a squirrel, whose dark
red fur blurs in evening static.
He trees him, paw on trunk, barks,
gives up, saunters to yard's edge.
Squirrel shakes his red fist, waits.

The Lab, coiled at corner fence,
says with eyes, what if
I sailed over these thin links?
Then jumps, clears links,
looks back, knows.

Squirrel shuffles down, safe,
as the black dog barrels
downstreet to tree others.

SHOWING OFF

This squirrel
is smart,
eyes me,
levers
precisely
onto the ledge
of the narrow
sparrow feeder
swinging
from his tree.

He steps
  misses
    drops
      into bluestem.

He emerges
moments later
ruffled red:
a perfectly
executed
performance.

To see how Surrealists
for Caryn Mirriam-Goldberg

ease the pressure we all gather
by virtue of living, take
your watch from the nightstand.
Carry it into that wide ship's hold
of thundered sky, and hold it
aloft, a lightening lightning rod
with open and welcoming hands:
your own turning, circular
hot spot, your transient metal heart.

RECIPE, CONDENSED

How many tons of rain
we'll need for the perfect pillar
of hackle-tightening super-
cumulus night terror: take
that amount, eyeball
and pour, lifting
the bucket carefully
with your knees. Whip all this
into a pillar (see above), and
wait. The moment has come
to break a few eggs.

WATCHING SKY
for Thomas Fox Averill

Mornings, this farmhouse
echoes dusty silence
up to where the air
is papery as onion skin,
and every cloud
shudders like a gong.

We wait
for our myths to subside:
ancient prairie bruin,
Fenris, the goat chariots
no one rides. We hold
our breath. The world
starts to turn.

Bruin: *Arctodus simus*, a species of bear appearing in North America during the middle Pleistocene, some 800,000 years ago.

Fenris: A monstrous wolf in Norse mythology. Foretold to cause the death of Odin upon the occurrence of Ragnarök.

Goat chariots: In Norse mythology, two goats—Tanngrisnir and Tanngnjóstr (Toothgrinder and Toothgnasher)—pulled the god Thor's chariot.

Home

The kitchen window I looked through
after first moving in to this breaking place
has become host to an ominous black bird,
and none of us know its name.

It made the old frame rattle
like a smoker's broken lung at evening
as I carved sweet potatoes for dinner
to fry with other like vegetables.

And one wonders whether this bird
would taste any good if I added garlic
and a little oil and invited it, featherless,
into the frying pan.

This morning I saw the frame sag
out from the house, found an entry point
where the bird had stuffed a telephone book
and folded a paperback bible

somehow for a nest. Later I watched it
lift up through that larynx of rotting wood.
No doubt it will be back to stay.

ELEGY

This poem is about the blades
of Kansas windmills, their
frenetic chop of air
that slices shadows thin
as reason while we wait
at the edge of our field
in the dusking sky.

This poem subverts
the pastoral, nostalgia
free of hindsight,
our easiest caking agent,
with all the pragmatisms
inherent in the term.

This poem is a warning
to all who think gophers
don't leave holes, whose
naked ankles stand
eager to swim
the opened earth.

This poem believes
in extinction, knows
blades and grass keep
secrets just like us.

ELMER HAS THE PERFECT TRUCK

to sell me, just what I've been
looking for, and he says,
don't sweat it, you can trust me.

This truck, Elmer tells me,
still has its own original
cigarette lighter, and so what
that you don't smoke. It still
makes this truck worth more.

This truck has power windows,
and AC so cold
you'll never feel passion again.

This truck's tires are bold
enough to trample into dirt
any regrets you might have
about life before trucks.

Elmer tells me the price, and I
wake to pedestrian morning,
yearning for a better deal.

Driving Together

BUYING THE FORD

The morning you needed a car
we combed the papers
for the best cheap automatic
sedan we could find, and
even if it had a little rust
on the roof or if the doors
rattled a little or if we had
to evict a small family
of our least favorite small animals
it would be okay, because you
had places to go.

Only after we found it
did the owner tell us
that his little two-door Ford
was a manual. No matter,
you said, we can learn
to drive stick, I've always
needed to learn to drive
stick. And so we bought
the sleek black thing,
rust spots burning in the sun
like eyes
        when we coaxed
it down into the street.

We sputtered our narrow way
to the intersection's edge
and when you stalled it
we could feel the car waiting.
At our backs, dust
from a thousand other tires
held its own breath and
hung in the air like love.

ABLUTION

The black walnut by the porch
holds no robins today.
The usual jays fight in other branches.
Blue-gray cirrus hold back the sun
from its warming of the gravel,
and heavy in that craw
sits our two-door Ford.
Dawn beads watery eyes
on the windshield.

We read these omens over,
wind down wooden steps
headlong into the clean tang
of retreating rain.

First Weekend After Snow: Emporia, KS

we wake late, yawn deep,
press coffee, wait, drink.
Overhead through trees:
broad brackets full of geese.

Later in full sun
we drag Commercial
and Sixth. Our hands
make waves out windows
and we rumble fast as spring
into the last of Sunday,
its wide sky.

After Long John Silver's

you still had an urge for adventure, one
we apparently couldn't fill with hush puppies
and thick-cut lightly salted fries (and dipping
anything here in vinegar is disgusting,
you were always sure to tell me. That's not
adventure, that's some sort of perversion).
We crumpled our wrappers, lobbed them
at the trashcan, waved to the pimply cashier
behind the counter, and made our way out
to the parking lot. Your little two-door Ford
squatted there in the lightly falling rain,
ready to jump out at the street, crunch it
under hard tires, take its wallet, leave it
in the dust. You said, let's go
faster than we have the whole day, I'm ready.

This Ford, haggled down three hundred bucks
from asking price, showed red wires
through where it used to hold a radio.
Power steering was a long-forgotten dream,
the reservoir a ghost town tucked beside the engine.
Air conditioning was blasphemy or witch craft,
a mechanical betrayal against the god of older cars.
We rolled down the windows, and light rain
glazed the gray upholstery, shined the hood
like our fish-greased fingers
as we buckled ourselves in. On the street,
rain skittered on the windshield
and whipped out behind us like a silver tail
when you opened the engine up to see
what it could do, to go faster
than we ever had before.

SEMIOTICS

The first time we try anything
in the back of our little two-door
Ford it's winter, and no matter
how we face each other, the roof
slopes low like a matron
over our heads. Frosted windshield
knifes at our backs. We declare
the evening a stalemate,
and the coupe, vindicated,
settles deeper into Kansas snow.

AT THE END OF GRADUATE SCHOOL

My wife paints in acrylic, liquid plastic
on old shirts draped on pressboard, on the floor.
Look here, Alex says. See how this gray tee
takes the paint like it isn't even there.
She flings it from brush to that shirt.
Paint hangs to the surface, then sinks
quick out of sight, and I think
of the park at the end of our town
where we ran off last year, told no one,
arrived earlier than our minister and witnesses.
Where my parents scattered my brother
two dozen years before, when he didn't
borrow over three hours from our world.
Alex asks me to help her finish the project.
I take the brush she holds out to me. We sit
together on the floor, and move our hands
across old cotton still vibrant as a veil.

Waking after the Wreck

Hutchinson, Kansas, 2012

Lady cop knocked
on cracked eggshell windshield,
mouthed, can   you   get out?

Pried driver door open over
broken airbag yolk. Across
the street the big truck rumbled,

driver pacing dark pavement;
passenger slumped in their seat,
crumpled, asleep.

Back of my car
undercarriage tumbled easy
into nighttime Kansas street.

Get Lost

Tonight is not
the night for listening

to what anyone has to say,
so when next you drive anywhere

at all, wrench that GPS
from your dashboard, and

throw the damn thing out. That's
why we have paper maps, big paper

maps with beat-up creases
you can touch. Maybe

if lucky no one will ever find
that GPS, and you'll roll

slowly through the craggy road
actually thinking, but

not too hard about where
you are now, and why

you'd need to be anywhere
but there.

AFTER A CRASH

How ambulances lapse
    into silence
    (not doctor visits
    or cat scans or therapy)
after air bags
    knock you to sleep
  in the driver's seat

how a truck fender
    can fold a door in
      like foil
  and can spill your car
toward the only
    culvert in town
      without a fence

(how now you flinch
    each time anyone
      turns left, stoplight
        or not toward you)

that whistle (really a scream)
    is how you sound
when others hear you
    only once the steaming car
      is stopped

only once the cops
    pry open your door
      can you hear your voice
        again for the first time

        like a kettle on fire

SOUTH

LOUISIANA AUBADE

Businessmen,
dark-suit morning-shades men,
crowd community coffee counters,
round copper in loafers:
small suns in brown leather.

When to Run from a Hurricane

Morning conversation at McNeese State University, August 2016

Even though it's sometimes safer to go north
as far as possible, mandatory evacuation
doesn't mean you *have* to leave. Really,
if your home is elevated it might be enough
to sit there for a while in the dark

when the power goes out—and it *will*
go out—and the neighbor's truck floats
past your living room. When it gets hot
just remember that sweating is good for you,
far better than an August power bill.

Does it make me a terrible person
to hope that the Carolinas or maybe Florida
will get the worst of it, so we can say
our streets are dry and nothing but the usual?

Afterward we can all walk outside
and say that things are normal, that
next time will certainly happen
somewhere else, like next times always do.

YARDWORK

After two straight days of constant rain
our big-wheeled mulcher lies asleep
in the ebb and flow of the yard. I suppose
it's my duty to keep this grass in haircuts
or the neighbors will whine through the walls,
worse than their dogs. See
how the yard has a precise demarcation,
a crease of grass so fine where
they've trimmed it just so, letting me know
where I must cut and where to pass by.

See how the wheels line up just
over the edge of that last-cut path,
weaving in those neat rows.
See how the sliced blades braid
down like ropes to keep us here
while the motor pulls forward.

DEAD MAN FINGERS

Gulf crabs, when captured, mean business
all the time. Tempered in big kettles,
they crawl over each other in the blind dark
until somebody lifts the lid. They are
prepared to break off their own arms
should they be lifted free of the mélange.
My wife's uncle takes eighteen
out of the store's big pot. They fight him
all the way to his burlap sack,
tiny mouths cursing in their secret language.

Wayne pins the arm of one big crab,
claw to carapace. He snaps
the other arm off like an icicle,
then flips it over on the big metal drum
we've gathered around. Before
you take its back off, he says,
act fast with that second arm.
Just like that, the crab is spinning
on the drum, armless, silent.
Its tiny mouth has stopped.

Wayne presses a palm
to the big crab's shell,
pulls at the ridged edge,
and it opens like a box,
unhinged; we see
the flesh of it, and cringe.

It has dark and feathered structures
near its eyes. Wayne calls them
dead man fingers, scrapes them
out. He says they'll kill us
if we don't get rid of them
right away. These gray digits
fall beside the empty shell
that sits beside this thing
that was a crab.

We cannot look away.
We reach into the sack
and pull more onto the drum.

AT THE COURT OF TWO SISTERS

Downtown New Orleans, January 2017

I haven't seen these streets in over a decade,
the bluesy, vibrating pavement capped by
some of the country's oldest buildings, and Taryn,
our guide who has lived here for years, says it hasn't
rained in weeks, so we'll want to avoid the puddles.
Further in, there are more people dressed in silver paint.
Gas lamps sputter and burn against the dark.

In a bar a band grinds out "Hoochie Coochie Man."
The guitar player deep in his gravelly voice
watches me watch him play, and nods through smoke.
On Rue Bourbon we stare at the sign that has seen
so much, drunken decades of brawls and hoodoo
that have faded its black finish.

At the Court we walk under a wisteria canopy
strung with lights, a single draping tree, and Taryn says
good wishes here protect you from what this town can do.
We throw corroded pennies in the well. Then we weave
back to the street, full of good luck and trouble,
and the old town tightens back around us.

When Next We Meet

CATHARSIS

A taxi driver clears his meter
on a Kansas street.

A honeybee cleans
its legs of pollen.

Small fish float, frozen,
in a thousand shallow ponds.

A preacher collects his sermon
from the lectern.

Somewhere in the Flint Hills,
a coyote howls,

his ears alert, his eyes
full of wind and moon.

FINDING YOURSELF

When it becomes night in the Midwest
will you be the one who dances
through wheat fields with a Mason jar,
building his own lamp?

Will you become the hum of cicadas
coaxing loved ones to sleep,
holding together their dreams
like feather pillows,
harvest moon and sky?

Will you build and burn a bonfire
and sing into the night,
and find animals
and wishes in smoke,
or lines for poems?

Driving Together

NOTES

"Replay": This poem was inspired by Latin American poetic concepts of rebirth.

"Mountains": All of these stories are the absolute truth.

Universal Solvents: The poems in this section focus on Cody William Sheldon, my identical twin brother, who died three hours after our birth on November 20, 1991. I miss him daily.

"Brother": The epigraph for this poem is taken from "Excerpts from the Mariposa Letters" by Jimmy Santiago Baca, in *Singing at the Gates: Selected Poems* (Grove Press, 2015). I'm glad to have shared dinner and good conversation with Jimmy in the fall of 2015, and to have gleaned inspiration from him for this poem.

"In Kansas": The salt mine of this poem is now Strataca Salt Museum in Hutchinson, Kansas. The museum, which sits 650 feet below ground, houses Hollywood props and other artifacts, like costumes from the films *Star Wars* and *Gone with the Wind*.

"Red-Tails": My wife and I have made a habit of counting hawks when on road trips. Once, en route to Mississippi, we counted some forty red-tails while passing through eastern Kansas.

"Discovering": This poem was inspired by the poetry of William Stafford, Kansas poet and Consultant in Poetry to the Library of Congress.

"Satori": This title is also the word for sudden enlightenment, as in a metaphorical lightning strike. Or a literal one, I suppose.

PUBLICATION CREDITS

I am grateful to the editors of the following publications, in which these poems, sometimes in other versions, first appeared:

Coal City Review: "Mountains"
Cybersoleil Literary Journal: "My Father Teaches Me to Shave" and "Red-Tails"
DIG Baton Rouge: "Yardwork"
The Dos Passos Review: "Discovering"
The Emporia Gazette: "Elmer has the perfect truck"
Kansas Time+Place: "For Kansas Poets"
Konza: "Watching Sky" and "Home"
I-70 Review: "Replay," "Brother," and "Scar"
The Midwest Quarterly: "Gravity" and "Get Lost"
MockingHeart Review: "Guitar" and "After Long John Silver's"
The Prairie Journal of Canadian Literature: "Catharsis"
Quiddity International Literary Journal: "Universal Solvents" and "Sea Ghosts of Kansas"
Quivira: "Elegy" and "Finding Yourself"
Symphony in the Flint Hills Field Journal: "Code"
Thorny Locust: "Discovering a Lost Twin," "Showing Off," and "Recipe, Condensed"
Tin Lunchbox Review: "Dead Man Fingers"
Tittynope Zine: "Semiotics" and "At the End of Graduate School"
150 Kansas Poems: "Lemons," "August," and "In Kansas"

"If You're Listening," "Photo of Brother," "Buying the Ford," and "Waking After the Wreck" first appeared in the chapbook *Traumas* (Yellow Flag Press, 2017).

"Negotiations" and "To See How Surrealists" were first published in the anthology *365 Poems in 365 Days*, edited by Roy Beckemeyer, James Benger, Dan Pohl, and Diane Wahto.

"Universal Solvents" was nominated for the Pushcart Prize by *Quiddity International Literary Journal*.

"For Kansas Poets" was written with William Sheldon. It's always great to work with you, Dad. Cool up.

Acknowledgments

My deep gratitude to Thomas Fox Averill, Sammie Bellavia, James Benger, Brian Daldorph, Du Peng, Harley Elliott, Amy Fleury, Jessica Frank, J. Bruce Fuller, Albert Goldbarth, Sadie Hutchison, John Jenkinson, Kelli Scott Kelley, Ted Kooser, Marcia Lawrence, Keagan LeJeune, Ashlee Lhamon, Denise Low, Deb and Terry Maxwell, Max McCoy, Ronda Miller, Lisa Moritz, Stephen and Taryn Möller Nicoll, David Palmer, Dan Pohl, Jeanette Powers, Kevin Rabas, Michelle Romero, Kim Stafford, Patricia Traxler, and Trudy Zimmerman, friends all, for your friendship, for your belief in my writing, and for your own good work. Thanks especially to Ruth Awad, Xánath Caraza, Steven Hind, Allison Joseph, Caryn Mirriam-Goldberg, Amy Sage Webb, and Kevin Rabas, for their clear-eyed, thoughtful assessments of these poems.

    Love and gratitude always to my family far and near, eternal pillars of love and support.

    Thanks as well to Tracy Million Simmons and Meadowlark Books for believing in these poems.

ABOUT THE AUTHOR

TYLER ROBERT SHELDON is the author of the chapbooks *Consolation Prize* (Finishing Line Press, 2018), *Traumas* (Yellow Flag Press, 2017), and *First Breaths of Arrival* (Oil Hill Press, 2016). He received the 2016 Charles E. Walton Essay Award, and his poetry has been nominated for the Pushcart Prize. His writing has appeared in *The Midwest Quarterly, The Los Angeles Review, Quiddity International Literary Journal, The Dos Passos Review, Coal City Review*, and other venues. He holds an MA in English from Emporia State University. Tyler lives in Baton Rouge, and is married to the artist Alexandria Arceneaux.

WWW.MEADOWLARK-BOOKS.COM

Specializing in Books by Authors from the Heartland since 2014

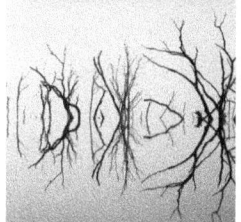

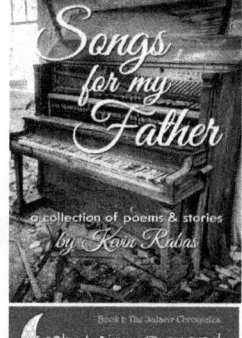
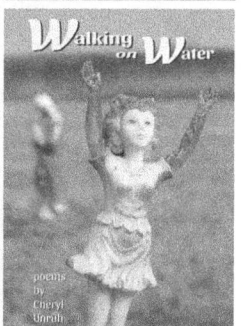

www.ingramcontent.com/pod-product-compliance
Lightning Source LLC
Chambersburg PA
CBHW051701090426
42736CB00013B/2491